What Is the Trinity?

A study of God in three persons

1

What Is The Trinity?

Written by Marcia Stoner

Susan Heinemann, Production Editor
Keitha Vincent, Designer

Art Credits—pp. 7–9, 11, 17, 25–26: © Shutterstock;
pp. 10, 16, 23: © Chuck Gonzales;
pp. 19, 21: Randy Wollenmann, © 2004, 2011 Cokesbury

ISBN-13: 978-1-426-74211-8
PACP00989033-01

12 13 14 15 16 17 18 19 20 21 - 10 9 8 7 6 5 4 3 2 1

Manufactured in the United States of America

CONTENTS

4

What Is?

So, what is the Trinity? The Trinity is a very important Christian belief. It is also the most difficult to truly understand.

The Trinity is a description of how God works in the world. It is called "God in three persons." This does not mean that there are three Gods, but rather that we experience God in three different ways.

Try the exercise on page 6 to learn more about the three ways we experience God.

Also, read about the three forms of water on page 7 and the Shamrock story on pages 8 and 9 to learn more about God in three persons.

Understanding the Trinity takes a long time, and that's OK. The Trinity is how we experience and relate to God. Any really good relationship takes a lot of interaction to develop and maintain. Our relationship with God is worth it.

Enjoy the journey.

GOD IN THREE PERSONS

What are the three persons of God? Choose the words that finish each statement.

One person of the Trinity is God who acts, created us, loves us, takes care of us, and lets us know when we've done wrong. This person of the Trinity is known as the _____.

BROTHER

CARETAKER

FATHER

TEACHER

One person of the Trinity is the one who came to us on earth so that we would know and experience the love of God in human form. This person of the Trinity is the _____.

YOUNGER SISTER

SON

COACH

HELPER

One person of the Trinity is the one who gives us the desire and the strength inside of ourselves to live as God wants us to live. This person of the Trinity is the _____.

SUPER HERO

INSIDE MAN

HAPPINESS GIVER

HOLY SPIRIT

(Answers are on p. 29.)

Three States of Water

There is one way to help you think about the three persons of God. It's not a perfect analogy, but it gives us a beginning place.

Think about water. How do you experience water?

1. When we take a bath in it, drink it, or brush our teeth with it, we

   experience water as a _____.
   IIUDLQ

2. When we boil water in a tea kettle and it begins to whistle or

   when we sit in a sauna, we experience water as _____.
   SMATE

3. When we freeze water to put in lemonade to cool it down or

   when we go play hockey on water, we experience water as

   _____ or a _____.
   EIC   **LDSIO**

   We also experience God in three different ways.

(Our answers are on p. 29.)

The Shamrock

Think Ireland. Think three-leaf clover. The three-leaf clover of Ireland is called the shamrock.

Now think about the Trinity and Saint Patrick.

This is the story of how the shamrock (which some people call a trefoil) became a symbol of the Trinity.

About four hundred years after Christ, there was a missionary named Patrick. He came before the Irish king. He wanted the king to understand Christianity, so he attempted to explain the Trinity to the Irish king.

However, this explanation only made the king confused and angry, because he could not understand the idea of "three persons in one."

Patrick bent down, picked a shamrock, and showed it to the king. Patrick showed the king that one perfect leaf could have three perfect parts.

Patrick asked the king whether the shamrock was one leaf or three. The king could not decide.

This is how the king came to understand that something so complex and unbelievable as the Trinity could be true.

From that day to the present, the shamrock has been a symbol of the Trinity—God in three persons, yet only one God.

I Believe, Part 1

The Apostle's Creed is a statement of faith of Christians. It will help us understand Christian beliefs about the Trinity.

For this first part of the statement, fill in the missing consonants to discover more about one of the persons of God.

The missing consonants are listed on page 11.

I believe in ___ O ___ the ___ A ___ ___ E ___

A ___ ___ I ___ ___ ___ Y, ___ A ___ E ___ of

___ E A ___ E ___ and E A ___ ___ ___.

From the Apostles' Creed, traditional version

Choose from these consonants to complete the first part of the Apostles' Creed.

Hint: Cross out each consonant as you use it.

D F G G H H H H K L
M M N R R R T T T V

(Answers are on p. 29.) 11

God and

God is the Trinity. (Remember that it says, "God in three persons.") So, what does the Bible tell us about God? Why is God important to us? Discovering some of these things for ourselves is what helps us develop a deeper relationship with God.

The Bible tells us a lot about God, so we can discover a lot about God by reading Scripture.

Match the Scripture to the statement about God. To make it a little more challenging, we put in one statement that does NOT describe God.

○ **Genesis 1:1-27**   ○ **Psalm 11:1**

○ **Psalm 136:1**   ○ **1 John 4:7-9**

○ **John 3:16**   ○ **Micah 6:8**

the Bible

O God loves us so much that God willingly made a sacrifice in order to bring us closer and offer us eternal life.

O When afraid or lonely, we can take refuge in God.

O God is the Creator.

O We know exactly how God requires us to live.

O God forgives us only if we confess in front of the congregation.

O We learn how to truly love from God because love is from God.

O God's love for us is constant and never changing. (That's the meaning of "steadfast.")

(Answers are on p. 29.)

I Believe, Part 2

To discover what Christians believe about another part of the Trinity, find the words in the wordsearch and then discover where they go below.

I believe in __ __ __ __ __   __ __ __ __ __ __, his only __ __ __,

our __ __ __ __, who was conceived by the Holy Spirit,

__ __ __ __ of the Virgin Mary, __ __ __ __ __ __ __ __ __ under

Pontius Pilate, was __ __ __ __ __ __ __ __ __ __, died, and was

__ __ __ __ __ __; he descended to the __ __ __ __.

On the __ __ __ __ __ day he __ __ __ __ again;

he __ __ __ __ __ __ __ __ __ into __ __ __ __ __ __,

and sitteth at the __ __ __ __ __   __ __ __ __ of God the Father

Almighty; from thence he will come to __ __ __ __ __ __ the quick

and the dead.

From the Apostles' Creed, traditional version

```
C  K  K  N  L  O  R  D  U
Y  R  T  J  R  N  Q  N  S
T  L  U  H  E  O  T  A  U
H  H  J  C  G  S  B  H  F
R  E  I  U  I  I  U  S  F
O  M  A  R  D  F  R  S  E
S  B  H  V  D  G  I  Q  R
E  C  D  A  E  D  E  E  E
R  A  S  C  E  N  D  E  D
```

ASCENDED	CRUCIFIED	JESUS	ROSE
BORN	DEAD	JUDGE	SON
BURIED	HAND	LORD	SUFFERED
CHRIST	HEAVEN	RIGHT	THIRD

(Answers are on p. 30.)

The Bible has many descriptions about Jesus that begin with the words "I am." Can you finish these sayings by choosing the words from the list?

• I am the _____ of life.

• I am the _____ of the world.

• I am the good _____.

• I am the _____ and the _____.

• I am the _____ and the _____, the first and the last, the _____ and the _____.

• I am the _____ and _____ of David.

16 • I am the _____ _____ _____.

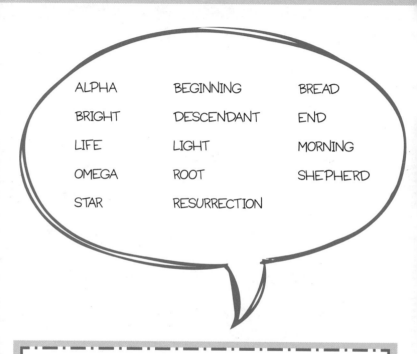

ALPHA   BEGINNING   BREAD

BRIGHT   DESCENDANT   END

LIFE   LIGHT   MORNING

OMEGA   ROOT   SHEPHERD

STAR   RESURRECTION

Here are the Scripture references to help out:

John 6:35   John 10:11   Revelation 22:13

John 8:12   John 11:25   Revelation 22:16

(Answers are on p. 31.)

Names for Jesus

In each word, cross out the letters that spell *Jesus* and write the new word or phrase on the blank. A Scripture reference is under each line. (The first one is done for you as an example.)

KIJNGEOSFKIUNSGS <········>

King of Kings
_____

JMEESSSUSIAH <········>

_____
Matthew 1:1-2

SOJNOESFDAUVSID <········>

_____
Matthew 20:31

SJOENSOFGUOSD <········>

_____
John 3:35-36

LORJDEOFSLORUDSS <········>

_____
Revelation 19:16

 18

(Answers are on p. 31.)

SYMBOLS OF JESUS

Here are a few symbols of Jesus.

The Alpha and Omega
(the beginning and end)

The Chi Rho
(Greek monogram for *Jesus Christ*)

Jesus Monogram
(the first three letters in the Greek word for *Jesus*)

Acrostic for the Greek word
ICHTHUS (fish):
I Jesus
CH Christ
TH God
U Son
S Savior

I Believe, Part 3

The third person of the Trinity is the one that gives us the power to live as Christians even when things get rough. Circle every fifth letter below, starting in the center, to discover the name of this person of the Trinity.

(Answers are on p. 31.)

Holy Spirit Symbols

The symbol of the Holy Spirit is the descending dove.

Why is the dove descending? Because the Holy Spirit comes to us from God. The descending dove is used as a symbol of baptism. At Jesus' baptism, "he saw the Spirit of God descending like a dove" (Matthew 3:16).

It is also one of the symbols of Pentecost (the birthday of the church). It was at Pentecost when the Holy Spirit descended to Jesus' disciples.

The flame is a symbol of he descent of the Holy Spirit on the disciples at Pentecost.

WHAT DO YOU KNOW ABOUT THE SPIRIT?

Make an *X* before each statement below that is about the Holy Spirit. If you need help, use the Scripture references on page 23.

____ The symbol for the Holy Spirit is a descending dove. This is a symbol of God coming to us.

____ The Holy Spirit gives us the power to be good witnesses for Christ.

____ The Holy Spirit gives us super powers.

____ Because of the Spirit, we all have the same gifts and abilities.

____ We all receive the same Spirit, but we have a variety of gifts (talents).

____ The fruit of the Spirit is jealousy, anger, quarrels, envy, and drunkenness.

____ The fruit of the Spirit is love, joy, peace, patience, kindness, generosity, faithfulness, gentleness, and self-control.

(Answers are on p. 31.)

Scripture references

Matthew 3:16

Acts 1:8

1 Corinthians 12: 4-11

Galatians 5:20

Galatians 5:22-23

Symbols of the Trinity

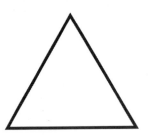

The equilateral triangle with three equal sides and three equal angles represents the three equal persons of the Trinity.

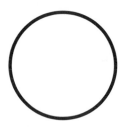

The circle is the symbol of eternity. There is no beginning or end.

When you put the circle representing eternity inside the triangle representing the Trinity, you have a symbol of the Trinity representing the unending Trinity.

The shamrock represents the Trinity as three persons of one God.

The iris has three upright petals and three petals that drape downward. Often in art, the third petal at the top is not shown because it would be at the back of the iris. Each set of three petals represents the Trinity.

The Triquetra is made by placing arcs together to form a type of triangle. The arcs are always of equal size. This symbolizes the equality of the three persons of the Trinity.

These overlapping circles represent the three natures of God—Father, Son, and Holy Spirit. Circles are used to represent the unending nature of God.

Use what you've discovered about symbols in this book to complete the Clueless Crossword.

Clueless Crossword

(Answers are on p. 32.)

27

What I Believe

Write your own beliefs about the Trinity. Put what you personally believe in your own words.

ABOUT GOD:
_____

_____

_____

ABOUT JESUS:
_____

_____

_____

ABOUT THE HOLY SPIRIT:
_____

_____

_____

ANSWERS

God in Three Persons (p. 6): Father, Son, Holy Spirit

Three States of Water (p. 7): liquid, steam, ice (solid)

I Believe, Part 1 (p. 10): I believe in God the Father Almighty, maker of heaven and earth.

God and the Bible (pp. 12–13):
God loves us so much that God willingly made a sacrifice in order to bring us closer and offer us eternal life. (John 3:16)
When afraid or lonely, we can take refuge in God. (Psalm 11:1)
God is the Creator. (Genesis 1:1-27)
We know exactly how God requires us to live. (Micah 6:8)
We learn how to truly love from God because love is from God. (John 4:7-9)
God's love for us is constant and never changing. (Psalm 136:1)

I Believe, Part 2 (pp. 14–15):

I believe in Jesus Christ, his only Son, our Lord,
 who was conceived by the Holy Spirit,
  born of the Virgin Mary,
  suffered under Pontius Pilate,
  was crucified, died, and was buried;
  he descended to the dead.
  On the third day he rose again;
   he ascended into heaven,
     and sitteth at the right hand of God the Father Almighty;
     from thence he shall come to judge the quick and the dead.

C	K	K	N	L	O	R	D	U
Y	R	T	J	R	N	Q	N	S
T	L	U	H	E	O	T	A	U
H	H	J	C	G	S	B	H	F
R	E	I	U	I	I	U	S	F
O	M	A	R	D	F	R	S	E
S	B	H	V	D	G	I	Q	R
E	C	D	A	E	D	E	E	E
R	A	S	C	E	N	D	E	D

I Am (pp. 16–17):
    I am the BREAD of life. (John 6:35)
    I am the LIGHT of the world. (John 8:12)
    I am the good SHEPHERD. (John 10:11)
    I am the RESURRECTION and LIFE. (John 11:25)
    I am the ALPHA and OMEGA, the FIRST and the LAST, the
      BEGINNING and the END. (Revelation 22:13)
    I am the ROOT and DESCENDENT of David. (Revelation 22:16)
    I am the BRIGHT MORNING STAR. (Revelation 22:16)

Names for Jesus (p. 18): Messiah, Son of David, Son of God,
  Lord of Lords

I Believe, Part 3 (p. 20): Holy Spirit

What Do You Know About the Spirit? (p. 22):
    Statements about the Holy Spirit:
      The symbol for the Holy Spirit is a descending dove.
      The Holy Spirit gives us the power to be good witnesses for Christ.
      We all receive the same Spirit, but we have a variety of gifts.
      The fruit of the Spirit is love, joy, peace, patience, kindness,
        generosity, faithfulness, gentleness, and self-control.

Clueless Crossword (p. 27):

							D¹	O²	V	E³
								M		N
					S⁴			E		T
					H			G		W
		T⁵			A⁶	L	P	H	A	I
		R			M					N
T⁷	R	I	Q	U	E	R	T	A		E
		A			R	O				D
		N			C⁸	H	I⁹	R	H	O
		G			K		R			
		L				C¹⁰	I	R	C	L	E
		E					S			

32